The World's
Greatest Collection of

# KNOCK

# KNOCK

# JOKES

and
## TONGUE
## TWISTERS

by
## BOB PHILLIPS

A Barbour Book

© Copyright MCMXCV by Barbour and Company, Inc.

ISBN 1-55748-650-6

Published by **BARBOUR AND COMPANY, INC.**
**P.O. BOX 719**
**UHRICHSVILLE, OH 44683**

Printed in the United States of America.

# KNOCK
# KNOCK
# JOKES

Knock knock.
Who's there?
*Abbot.*
Abbot who?
*Abbot you don't know who this is!*

* * *

Knock knock.
Who's there?
*Abe Lincoln.*
Abe Lincoln who?
*Dummy! Don't you know who Abe Lincoln is?*

* * *

Knock knock.
Who's there?
*Ach.*
Ach who?
*God bless you!*

* * *

Knock knock.
Who's there?
*A cheetah.*
A cheetah who?
*A cheetah never wins.*

Knock knock.
Who's there?
*Adam.*

Adam who?
*Adam up and get the total.*

\* \* \*

*Knock knock.*
Who's there?
*Adele.*
Adele who?
*Adele is where the farmer's in.*

\* \* \*

*Knock knock.*
Who's there?
*Adore.*
Adore who?
*Adore is between us. Open up.*

\* \* \*

*Knock knock.*
Who's there?
*Agatha.*
Agatha who?
*Agatha feeling you're fooling.*

\* \* \*

*Knock knock.*
Who's there?
*Ahead.*
Ahead who?
*Ahead is on your shoulders.*

\* \* \*

*Knock knock.*
Who's there?
*A herd.*
A herd who?
*A herd you were home, so I came over!*

\* \* \*

*Knock knock.*
Who's there?
*Aida.*
Aida who?
*Aida sandwich at recess time.*

\* \* \*

*Knock knock.*
Who's there?
*Akron.*
Akron who?
*Akron give you anything but love, baby.*

\* \* \*

*Knock knock.*
Who's there?
*Alaska.*
Alaska who?
*Alaska no questions. You tella no lies.*

\* \* \*

*Knock knock.*
Who's there?
*Alby.*

Alby who?
*Alby glad when school's over.*

\* \* \*

*Knock knock.*
Who's there?
*Alfred.*
Alfred who?
*Alfred the needle if you'll sew the button on.*

\* \* \*

*Knock knock.*
Who's there?
*Ali.*
Ali who?
*Ali Bama.*

\* \* \*

*Knock knock.*
Who's there?
*Alison.*
Alison who?
*Alison to the radio.*

\* \* \*

*Knock knock.*
Who's there?
*A little boy who can't reach the doorbell.*

\* \* \*

*Knock knock.*
Who's there?
*Allmen.*
Allmen who?
*Allmen act silly.*

\* \* \*

*Knock knock.*
Who's there?
*Allotta.*
Allotta who?
*Allotta noise you're making.*

\* \* \*

*Knock knock.*
Who's there?
*Althea.*
Althea who?
*Althea in my dreams.*

\* \* \*

*Knock knock.*
Who's there?
*Amos.*
Amos who?
*A mosquito bit me.*

\* \* \*

*Knock knock.*
Who's there?
*Andy.*
Andy who?

9

*And he bit me again.*

\* \* \*

*Knock knock.*
Who's there?
*Andrew.*
Andrew who?
*Andrew a picture of me today.*

\* \* \*

*Knock knock.*
Who's there?
*Anita.*
Anita who?
*Anita minute to think it over.*

\* \* \*

*Knock knock.*
Who's there?
*Annette.*
Annette who?
*Annette is needed to catch butterflies.*

\* \* \*

*Knock knock.*
Who's there?
*Annie.*
Annie who?
*Annie-body seen my lost dog?*

\* \* \*

*Knock knock.*
Who's there?
*Apollo.*
Apollo who?
*Apollo you anywhere if you blow in my ear!*

\* \* \*

*Knock knock.*
Who's there?
*Apricot.*
Apricot who?
*Apricot my key. Open up!*

\* \* \*

*Knock knock.*
Who's there?
*Archer.*
Archer who?
*Archer mother and father at home?*

\* \* \*

*Knock knock.*
Who's there?
*Arthur.*
Arthur who?
*Arthur mometer is broken.*

\* \* \*

*Knock knock.*
Who's there?
*Aster.*
Aster who?

*Aster yourself.*

\* \* \*

*Knock knock.*
Who's there?
*Astor.*
Astor who?
*Astor if she kept a diary.*

\* \* \*

*Knock knock.*
Who's there?
*Atom.*
Atom who?
*Atom N. Eve.*

\* \* \*

*Knock knock.*
Who's there?
*Attack.*
Attack who?
*Attack is sharp if you sit on it.*

\* \* \*

*Knock knock.*
Who's there?
*Augusta.*
Augusta who?
*Augusta wind blew my hat off!*

\* \* \*

*Knock knock.*
Who's there?
*Avenue.*
Avenue who?
*Avenue knocked on this door before?*

\* \* \*

*Knock knock.*
Who's there?
*Avon.*
Avon who?
*The Avon lady. Your doorbell isn't working.*

\* \* \*

*Knock knock.*
Who's there?
*Ax.*
Ax who?
*Ax your mother if you can come out and play.*

\* \* \*

*Knock knock.*
Who's there?
*Banana.*
Banana who?
*Knock knock.*
Who's there?
*Banana.*
Banana who?
*Knock knock.*
Who's there?
*Banana.*
Banana who?

*Knock knock.*
Who's there?
*Orange.*
Orange who?
*Orange you glad I didn't say banana again?*

\* \* \*

*Knock knock.*
Who's there?
*Bay.*
Bay who?
*Bay be face, you've got the cutest little baby face!*

\* \* \*

*Knock knock.*
Who's there?
*Be.*
Be who?
*Be down to get you in a taxi, honey.*

\* \* \*

*Knock knock.*
Who's there?
*Beckon.*
Beckon who?
*Beckon goes well with eggs.*

\* \* \*

*Knock knock.*
Who's there?
*Ben.*
Ben who?

*Ben down and tie my shoes, please.*

\* \* \*

*Knock knock.*
Who's there?
*Ben Hur.*
Ben Hur who?
*Ben Hur waiting for ten minutes.*

\* \* \*

*Knock knock.*
Who's there?
*Bob.*
Bob who?
*Bob, baa black sheep, have you any wool?*

\* \* \*

*Knock knock.*
Who's there?
*Boo-hoo.*
Boo-hoo who?
*Boo-hoo-hoo.*
Boo-hoo-hoo who?
*Boo-hoo-hoo-hoo.*
Boo-hoo-hoo-hoo who?
*Boo-hoo-hoo-hoo-hoo.*
Boo-hoo-hoo-hoo-hoo who?
*Stop it! You're breaking my heart!*

\* \* \*

*Knock knock.*
Who's there?

*Boop-boopie.*
Boop-boopie who?
*Boop-boopie doo.*

\* \* \*

*Knock knock.*
Who's there?
*Butch, Jimmy, and Joe.*
Butch, Jimmy, and Joe who?
*Butch your arms around me, Jimmy a kiss, or I'll Joe home.*

\* \* \*

*Knock knock.*
Who's there?
*Butcher.*
Butcher who?
*Butcher feet on the floor.*

\* \* \*

*Knock knock.*
Who's there?
*Butter.*
Butter who?
*Butter be home before midnight.*

\* \* \*

*Knock knock.*
Who's there?
*Butternut.*
Butternut who?
*Butternut try to pick up a skunk.*

\* \* \*

*Knock knock.*
Who's there?
*Bwana.*
Bwana who?
*Bwana hold your hand.*

\* \* \*

*Knock knock.*
Who's there?
*Caesar.*
Caesar who?
*Caesar jolly good fellow.*

\* \* \*

*Knock knock.*
Who's there?
*Cameron.*
Cameron who?
*Cameron film are what you need to take pictures.*

\* \* \*

*Knock knock.*
Who's there?
*Candy.*
Candy who?
*Candy door be opened? I want to get out.*

\* \* \*

*Knock knock.*
Who's there?

*Canine.*
Canine who?
*Canine, B-6, O-74. BINKO!*

\* \* \*

*Knock knock.*
Who's there?
*Canoe.*
Canoe who?
*Canoe help me with my homework?*

\* \* \*

*Knock knock.*
Who's there?
*Canoe.*
Canoe who?
*Canoe come out and play with me?*

\* \* \*

*Knock knock.*
Who's there?
*Cantaloupe.*
Cantaloupe who?
*Cantaloupe without a ladder.*

\* \* \*

*Knock knock.*
Who's there?
*Carfare.*
Carfare who?
*Carfare a cookie or a piece of pie?*

* * *

*Knock knock.*
Who's there?
*Carmen.*
Carmen who?
*Carmen get it.*

* * *

*Knock knock.*
Who's there?
*Cartoon.*
Cartoon who?
*Cartoon ups are necessary to*
keep your car running smoothly.

* * *

*Knock knock.*
Who's there?
*Catch.*
Catch who?
*Gesundheit!*

* * *

*Knock knock.*
Who's there?
*Catsup.*
Catsup who?
*Catsup a tree.*

* * *

*Knock knock.*

19

Who's there?
*Cayuse.*
Cayuse who?
*Cayuse your bathroom?*

* * *

*Knock knock.*
Who's there?
*Celeste.*
Celeste who?
*Celeste time I'll tell you a knock-knock joke.*

* * *

*Knock knock.*
Who's there?
*Celia.*
Celia who?
*Celia later.*

* * *

*Knock knock.*
Who's there?
*Chaise.*
Chaise who?
*Chaise him away.*

* * *

*Knock knock.*
Who's there?
*Chester.*
Chester who?
*Chester minute and I'll see.*

* * *

*Knock knock.*
Who's there?
*Choo-choo train.*
Choo-choo train who?
*Choo-choo trained the lion, but he had trouble getting the tiger to cooperate.*

* * *

*Knock knock.*
Who's there?
*Closure.*
Closure who?
*Closure mouth, I'm talking!*

* * *

*Knock knock.*
Who's there?
*Cock-a-doodle.*
Cock-a-doodle who?
*Are you a rooster?*

* * *

*Knock knock.*
Who's there?
*Colin.*
Colin who?
*Colin here, shut the window.*

* * *

21

*Knock knock.*
Who's there?
*Column.*
Column who?
*Column loud and clear.*

\* \* \*

*Knock knock.*
Who's there?
*Consumption.*
Comsumption who?
*Consumption be done about these knock-knock jokes?*

\* \* \*

*Knock knock.*
Who's there?
*Datsun.*
Datsun who?
*Datsun of mine is sure a little pest!*

\* \* \*

*Knock knock.*
Who's there?
*Deboy.*
Deboy who?
*Deboy is cute.*

\* \* \*

*Knock knock.*
Who's there?
*Deep.*
Deep who?

*Deep ends on who you were expecting.*

\*\*\*

*Knock knock.*
Who's there?
*Della.*
Della who?
*Della Katessen.*

\*\*\*

*Knock knock.*
Who's there?
*Dewey.*
Dewey who?
*Dewey have to listen to all this knocking?*

\*\*\*

*Knock knock.*
Who's there?
*Dick.*
Dick who?
*Dick 'em up, I'm a tongue-tied robber.*

\*\*\*

*Knock knock.*
Who's there?
*Diesel.*
Diesel who?
*Diesel be your last chance to open the door.*

\*\*\*

*Knock knock.*
Who's there?
*Dishes.*
Dishes who?
*Dishes me. Who ish you?*

* * *

*Knock knock.*
Who's there?
*Disjoint.*
Disjoint who?
*Disjoint is closed.*

* * *

*Knock knock.*
Who's there?
*Distress.*
Distress who?
*Distress hardly covers my knees.*

* * *

*Knock knock.*
Who's there?
*Divan.*
Divan who?
*Divan the bathtub — I'm drowning.*

* * *

*Knock knock.*
Who's there?
*Divan.*
Divan who?

*Divan the pool and go swimming.*

* * *

*Knock knock.*
Who's there?
*Doris.*
Doris who?
*Doris closed — that's why I knocked.*

* * *

*Knock knock.*
Who's there?
*Dozen.*
Dozen who?
*Dozen anybody want to let me in?*

* * *

*Knock knock.*
Who's there?
*Duke.*
Duke who?
*Duke the halls with boughs of holly.*

* * *

*Knock knock.*
Who's there?
*Duncan.*
Duncan who?
*Duncan doughnuts in your milk makes 'em soft.*

* * *

*Knock knock.*
Who's there?
*Dwayne.*
Dwayne who?
*Dwayne the bathtub, I'm dwowning.*

\* \* \*

*Knock knock.*
Who's there?
*Dynamite.*
Dynamite who?
*Dynamite play with us if we're good.*

\* \* \*

*Knock knock.*
Who's there?
*Eclipse.*
Eclipse who?
*Eclipse my hair in the barber shop.*

\* \* \*

*Knock knock.*
Who's there?
*Edsall.*
Edsall who?
*Edsall there is — there isn't anymore.*

\* \* \*

*Knock knock.*
Who's there?
*Egypt.*
Egypt who?

*Egypt me, call a cop.*

\* \* \*

*Knock knock.*
Who's there?
*Egypt.*
Egypt who?
*Egypt me when he gave me change!*

\* \* \*

*Knock knock.*
Who's there?
*Eileen.*
Eileen who?
*Eileen on a walking stick.*

\* \* \*

*Knock knock.*
Who's there?
*Eileen.*
Eileen who?
*Eileen over to tie my shoes.*

\* \* \*

*Knock knock.*
Who's there?
*Elder.*
Elder who?
*Elder in my arms all evening.*

\* \* \*

*Knock knock.*
Who's there?
*Elephants.*
Elephants who?
*Elephants Gerald, the singer.*

\* \* \*

*Knock knock.*
Who's there?
*Ellison.*
Ellison who?
*Ellison the alphabet after K.*

\* \* \*

*Knock knock.*
Who's there?
*Emerson.*
Emerson who?
*Emerson big eyes you've got, baby.*

\* \* \*

*Knock knock.*
Who's there?
*Ether.*
Ether who?
*Ether bunny.*

*Knock knock.*
Who's there?
*Hop.*
Hop who?
*Hop, hop way, Ether bunny gone.*

*Knock knock.*
Who's there?
*Cargo.*
Cargo who?
*Cargo beep and ran over the Ether bunny*

*Knock knock.*
Who's there?
*Boo.*
Boo who?
*Don't cry— Ether bunny be back next year.*

* * *

*Knock knock.*
Who's there?
*Etta.*
Etta who?
*Etta Kett.*

* * *

*Knock knock.*
Who's there?
*Eva.*
Eva who?
*Eva since yesterday I've been knocking.*

* * *

*Knock knock.*
Who's there?
*Eyewash.*
Eyewash who?
*Eyewash I had a million dollars.*

* * *

*Knock knock.*
Who's there?
*Fang.*
Fang who?
*Fang you very much.*

* * *

*Knock knock.*
Who's there?
*Ferry.*
Ferry who?
*Ferry tales can come true.*

* * *

*Knock knock.*
Who's there?
*Finish.*
Finish who?
*Finish it yourself.*

* * *

*Knock knock.*
Who's there?
*Fire engine.*
Fire engine who?
*Fire engine one and prepare for blast-off*

* * *

*Knock knock.*
Who's there?
*Formosa.*

Formosa who?
*Formosa the term I was absent from school.*

\* \* \*

*Knock knock.*
Who's there?
*Freeze.*
Freeze who?
*Freeze a jolly good fellow.*

\* \* \*

*Knock knock.*
Who's there?
*Gary.*
Gary who?
*Gary me back to old Virginny.*

\* \* \*

*Knock knock.*
Who's there?
*Gibbon.*
Gibbon who?
*Gibbon take if you want to get along in the world.*

\* \* \*

*Knock knock.*
Who's there?
*Gladys.*
Gladys who?
*Gladys Friday — how 'bout you?*

\* \* \*

*Knock knock.*
Who's there?
*Gopher.*
Gopher who?
*Gopher your gun, Marshal!*

\* \* \*

*Knock knock.*
Who's there?
*Gorilla.*
Gorilla who?
*Gorilla my dreams, I love you.*

\* \* \*

*Knock knock.*
Who's there?
*Gretta.*
Gretta who?
*Gretta long, little doggie, gretta long.*

\* \* \*

*Knock knock.*
Who's there?
*Habit.*
Habit who?
*Habit your way.*

\* \* \*

*Knock knock.*
Who's there?
*Hair.*

Hair who?
*Hair today and gone tomorrow.*

* * *

*Knock knock.*
Who's there?
*Hallo.*
Hallo who?
*Halloween.*

* * *

*Knock knock.*
Who's there?
*Hank.*
Hank who?
*Hank E. Chief.*

* * *

*Knock knock.*
Who's there?
*Harry.*
Harry who?
*Harry up, it's cold out here.*

* * *

*Knock knock.*
Who's there?
*Hatch.*
Hatch who?
*God bless you!*

* * *

*Knock knock.*
Who's there?
*Heel.*
Heel who?
*Heel be right back.*

* * *

*Knock knock.*
Who's there?
*Heidi.*
Heidi who?
*Heidi Ho!*

* * *

*Knock knock.*
Who's there?
*Hence.*
Hence who?
*Hence lay eggs.*

* * *

*Knock knock.*
Who's there?
*Henrietta.*
Henrietta who?
*Henrietta worm that was in his apple.*

* * *

*Knock knock.*
Who's there?
*Holly.*

Holly who?
*Holly Louya.*

\* \* \*

*Knock knock.*
Who's there?
*Honeydew and cantaloupe.*
Honeydew and cantaloupe who?
*Honeydew you love me? We cantaloupe now.*

\* \* \*

*Knock knock.*
Who's there?
*Howl.*
Howl who?
*Howl it be if I come to your house today?*

\* \* \*

*Knock knock.*
Who's there?
*Hugh.*
Hugh who?
*Hugh Mility.*

\* \* \*

*Knock knock.*
Who's there?
*Hugo.*
Hugo who?
*Wherever Hugo, I go, too.*

\* \* \*

*Knock knock.*
Who's there?
*Hume.*
Hume who?
*Hume do you expect?*

\* \* \*

*Knock knock.*
Who's there?
*Humphrey.*
Humphrey who?
*Humphrey ever blowing bubbles.*

\* \* \*

*Knock knock.*
Who's there?
*Idaho.*
Idaho who?
*Idaho my own name.*

\* \* \*

*Knock knock.*
Who's there?
*I don't know. I didn't open the door yet.*

\* \* \*

*Knock knock.*
Who's there?
*Imus.*
Imus who?
*Imus get out of this rain.*

* * *

*Knock knock.*
Who's there?
*Iona.*
Iona who?
*Iona new car.*

* * *

*Knock knock.*
Who's there?
*Ira.*
Ira who?
*Ira member Mama.*

* * *

*Knock knock.*
Who's there?
*Iran.*
Iran who?
*Iran all the way home.*

* * *

*Knock knock.*
Who's there?
*Ireland.*
Ireland who?
*Ireland you a quarter if you promise to pay me back.*

* * *

*Knock knock.*

Who's there?
*Isabel.*
Isabel who?
*Isabel out of order?*

* * *

*Knock knock.*
Who's there?
*Isadore.*
Isadore who?
*Isadore locked?*

* * *

*Knock knock.*
Who's there?
*Israeli.*
Israeli who?
*Israeli great to see you again.*

* * *

*Knock knock.*
Who's there?
*Ivan.*
Ivan who?
*Ivan to hold your hand.*

* * *

*Knock knock.*
Who's there?
*Ivan.*
Ivan who?
*Ivan working on the railroad, all the livelong day.*

* * *

*Knock knock.*
Who's there?
*Ivan.*
Ivan who?
*Ivan wanting to drop over.*

* * *

*Knock knock.*
Who's there?
*Ivy League.*
Ivy League who?
*Ivy League for every drop of rain that falls, a flower grows.*

* * *

*Knock knock.*
Who's there?
*Jacket.*
Jacket who?
*Jacket up if you've got a flat tire.*

* * *

*Knock knock.*
Who's there?
*Jess.*
Jess who?
*Jess little old me.*

* * *

*Knock knock.*

Who's there?
*Jose.*
Jose who?
*Jose, can you see, by the dawn's early light?*

* * *

*Knock knock.*
Who's there?
*Juicy.*
Juicy who?
*Juicy any ghosts in the haunted house?*

* * *

*Knock knock.*
Who's there?
*Juneau.*
Juneau who?
*Juneau the capital of Alaska?*

* * *

*Knock knock.*
Who's there?
*Kangar.*
Kangar who?
*You will find them in Australia.*

* * *

*Knock knock.*
Who's there?
*Karen.*
Karen who?
*Karen a bundle of bricks isn't much fun.*

* * *

*Knock knock.*
Who's there?
*Kay.*
Kay who?
*Kay sera sera.*

* * *

*Knock knock.*
Who's there?
*Kerch.*
Kerch who?
*Gesundheit!*

* * *

*Knock knock.*
Who's there?
*Ketchup.*
Ketchup who?
*Ketchup with me and I'll tell you.*

* * *

*Knock knock.*
Who's there?
*Ketchup.*
Ketchup who?
*Ketchup to her before she turns the corner.*

* * *

*Knock knock.*

Who's there?
*Kleenex.*
Kleenex who?
*Kleenex are prettier than dirty necks.*

\* \* \*

*Knock knock.*
Who's there?
*Leggo.*
Leggo who?
*Leggo the door—I wanna come in!*

\* \* \*

*Knock knock.*
Who's there?
*Lessen.*
Lessen who?
*Lessen here and I'll tell you a knock-knock joke.*

\* \* \*

*Knock knock.*
Who's there?
*Lettuce.*
Lettuce who?
*Lettuce pray.*

\* \* \*

*Knock knock.*
Who's there?
*Linda.*
Linda who?
*Linda me some money, please.*

* * *

*Knock knock.*
Who's there?
*Lion.*
Lion who?
*Lion on a cold slab can be deadly!*

* * *

*Knock knock.*
Who's there?
*Lion.*
Lion who?
*Lion down on the job, eh?*

* * *

*Knock knock.*
Who's there?
*Lionel.*
Lionel who?
*Lionel roar if you don't feed him.*

* * *

*Knock knock.*
Who's there?
*Litter.*
Litter who?
*Litter go.*

* * *

*Knock knock.*

Who's there?
*Little old lady.*
Little old lady who?
*I didn't know you could yodel!*

* * *

*Knock knock.*
Who's there?
*Lois.*
Lois who?
*Lois the opposite of high.*

* * *

*Knock knock.*
Who's there?
*Lyndon.*
Lyndon who?
*Lyndon Bridge is falling down.*

* * *

*Knock knock.*
Who's there?
*Major.*
Major who?
*Major ask, didn't I?*

* * *

*Knock knock.*
Who's there?
*Mandy.*
Mandy who?
*Mandy lifeboats — the ship is sinking!*

* * *

*Knock knock.*
Who's there?
*Marcella.*
Marcella who?
*Marcella's full of water. Call a plumber.*

* * *

*Knock knock.*
Who's there?
*Marsha.*
Marsha who?
*Marsha-mallow.*

* * *

*Knock knock.*
Who's there?
*Max.*
Max who?
*Max no difference. Let me in.*

* * *

*Knock knock.*
Who's there?
*Mayonnaise.*
Mayonnaise who?
*Mayonnaise have seen the glory of . . . .*

* * *

*Knock knock.*

Who's there?
*Me.*
Me who?
*Don't you know your name?*

* * *

*Knock knock.*
Who's there?
*Mecca.*
Mecca who?
*Mecca noise like a duck.*

* * *

*Knock knock.*
Who's there?
*Mississippi.*
Mississippi who?
*Mississippi and Mr. Sippy. Can we come in?*

* * *

*Knock knock.*
Who's there?
*Missy.*
Missy who?
*Missy-laneous.*

* * *

*Knock knock.*
Who's there?
*Monopoly.*
Monopoly who?
*Monopoly's bigger than your nopoly.*

* * *

*Knock knock.*
**Who's there?**
*Morris.*
Morris who?
*Morris Monday; next day's Tuesday.*

* * *

*Knock knock.*
**Who's there?**
*Moscow.*
Moscow who?
*Moscow gives more milk than Pa's cow.*

* * *

*Knock knock.*
**Who's there?**
*Mountie.*
Mountie who?
*Mountie horses and go for a ride.*

* * *

*Knock knock.*
**Who's there?**
*Mush.*
Mush who?
*Mush be twenty past eight.*

* * *

*Knock knock.*

Who's there?
*My panther.*
My panther who?
*My panther falling down. I need a belt.*

\* \* \*

*Knock knock.*
Who's there?
*My Tommy.*
My Tommy who?
*My Tommy aches.*

\* \* \*

*Knock knock.*
Who's there?
*Navajo.*
Navajo who?
*You'll Navajo until you open the door.*

\* \* \*

*Knock knock.*
Who's there?
*Needle.*
Needle who?
*Needle little money for the movies.*

\* \* \*

*Knock knock.*
Who's there?
*Newton.*
Newton who?
*Newton doing.*

\* \* \*

*Knock knock.*
Who's there?
*Nicholas.*
Nicholas who?
*Nicholas half as much as a dime.*

\* \* \*

*Knock knock.*
Who's there?
*Noah.*
Noah who?
*Noah good place to eat around here?*

\* \* \*

*Knock, knock.*
Who's there?
*Nobody.*
Thank goodness!

\* \* \*

*Knock knock.*
Who's there?
*Nobody. I'm just banging on the table.*

\* \* \*

*Knock knock.*
Who's there?
*November.*
November who?
*November when we used to tell knock-knock jokes?*

49

\* \* \*

*Knock knock.*
Who's there?
*Nunna.*
Nunna who?
*Nunna your business.*

\* \* \*

*Knock knock.*
Who's there?
*Odyssey.*
Odyssey who?
*Odyssey a dentist if your tooth hurts.*

\* \* \*

*Knock knock.*
Who's there?
*Olga.*
Olga who?
*Olga round to the back door.*

\* \* \*

*Knock knock.*
Who's there?
*Olive.*
Olive who?
*Olive you, too, honey.*

\* \* \*

*Knock knock.*

Who's there?
*Oliver.*
Oliver who?
*Oliver troubles will soon be over.*

* * *

*Knock knock.*
Who's there?
*Omen.*
Omen who?
*Omen river, O omen river.*

* * *

*Knock knock.*
Who's there?
*Orange.*
Orange who?
*Orange you ever going home?*

* * *

*Knock knock.*
Who's there?
*Orange.*
Orange who?
*Orange you glad I'm here?*

* * *

*Knock knock.*
Who's there?
*Orange.*
Orange who?
*Orange you glad there are knock-knock jokes?*

* * *

*Knock knock.*
Who's there?
*Orange juice.*
Orange juice who?
*Orange juice sorry you made me cry?*

* * *

*Knock knock.*
Who's there?
*Orson.*
Orson who?
*Orson wagon are parked outside.*

* * *

*Knock knock.*
Who's there?
*Osborn.*
Osborn who?
*Osborn down in Mississippi. Where were you born?*

* * *

*Knock knock.*
Who's there?
*Oscar.*
Oscar who?
*Oscar if she wants to go to the party.*

* * *

*Knock knock.*

Who's there?
*Oscar.*
Oscar who?
*Oscar if she loves me.*

\* \* \*

*Knock knock.*
Who's there?
*Oswald.*
Oswald who?
*Oswald mah gum.*

\* \* \*

*Knock knock.*
Who's there?
*Otto.*
Otto who?
*Otto know. I've got amnesia.*

\* \* \*

*Knock knock.*
Who's there?
*Pasture.*
Pature who?
*Pasture math test, didn't you?*

\* \* \*

*Knock knock.*
Who's there?
*Pecan.*
Pecan who?
*Pecan somebody your own size.*

\* \* \*

*Knock knock.*
Who's there?
*Peeper.*
Peeper who?
*Peeper and salt, that's who.*

\* \* \*

*Knock knock.*
Who's there?
*Pepper.*
Pepper who?
*Pepper up. She looks tired.*

\* \* \*

*Knock knock.*
Who's there?
*Perry.*
Perry who?
*Perry Scope.*

\* \* \*

*Knock knock.*
Who's there?
*Phil.*
Phil who?
*Phil 'er up with regular, please.*

\* \* \*

*Knock knock.*

Who's there?
*Phillip.*
Phillip who?
*Phillup the tub so I can take a bath.*

\* \* \*

*Knock knock.*
Who's there?
*Phyllis.*
Phyllis who?
*Phyllis in on the news.*

\* \* \*

*Knock knock.*
Who's there?
*Phyllis.*
Phyllis who?
*Phyllis pitcher with water, please.*

\* \* \*

*Knock knock.*
Who's there?
*Pocket.*
Pocket who?
*Pocket in the pocking lot.*

\* \* \*

*Knock knock.*
Who's there?
*Police.*
Police who?
*Police hurry up. It's chilly outside.*

* * *

*Knock knock.*
Who's there?
*Police.*
Police who?
*Police may I sit down?*

* * *

*Knock knock.*
Who's there?
*Police.*
Police who?
*Police stop telling knock-knock jokes.*

* * *

*Knock knock.*
Who's there?
*Possum.*
Possum who?
*Possum ketchup for my hamburger.*

* * *

*Knock knock.*
Who's there?
*Pressure.*
Pressure who?
*Pressure shirt.*

* * *

*Knock knock.*

Who's there?
*Radio.*
Radio who?
*Radio not, here I come.*

* * *

*Knock knock.*
Who's there?
*Red.*
Red who?
*Red pepper. Isn't that a hot one?*

* * *

*Knock knock.*
Who's there?
*Rhoda.*
Rhoda who?
*Rhoda boat across da lake.*

* * *

*Knock knock.*
Who's there?
*Ripsaw.*
Ripsaw who?
*Ripsaw you downtown yesterday.*

* * *

*Knock knock.*
Who's there?
*Rita.*
Rita who?
*Rita good book lately?*

\* \* \*

*Knock knock.*
Who's there?
*Robin.*
Robin who?
*Robin a coffin is dangerous.*
*You could be in grave trouble.*

\* \* \*

*Knock knock.*
Who's there?
*Robot.*
Robot who?
*Robot don't splash with the oars.*

\* \* \*

*Knock knock.*
Who's there?
*Roland.*
Roland who?
*Roland butter taste good.*

\* \* \*

*Knock knock.*
Who's there?
*Ron.*
Ron who?
*Ron faster, there's a witch after us.*

\* \* \*

*Knock knock.*
Who's there?
*Roseanne.*
Roseanne who?
*Roseanne the tulip are my favorite flowers.*

\* \* \*

*Knock knock.*
Who's there?
*Roxanne.*
Roxanne who?
*Roxanne shells were on the beach.*

\* \* \*

*Knock knock.*
Who's there?
*Saber.*
Saber who?
*Saber, she's drowning!*

\* \* \*

*Knock knock.*
Who's there?
*Sahara.*
Sahara who?
*Sahara you today?*

\* \* \*

*Knock knock.*
Who's there?
*Salmon.*
Salmon who?

*Salmon Jack are over at my house.*

* * *

*Knock knock.*
Who's there?
*Sam and Janet.*
Sam and Janet who?
*Sam and Janet evening, you will meet a stranger.*

* * *

*Knock knock.*
Who's there?
*Samoa.*
Samoa who?
*Samoa knock-knock jokes.*

* * *

*Knock knock.*
Who's there?
*Sandy.*
Sandy who?
*Sandy Claus!*

* * *

*Knock knock.*
Who's there?
*Santa Ana.*
Santa Anna who?
*Santa Ana gonna bring you anything
if you don't believe in him.*

* * *

*Knock knock.*
Who's there?
*Sarah.*
Sarah who?
*Sarah doctor in the house?*

\* \* \*

*Knock knock.*
Who's there?
*Scold.*
Scold who?
*Scold enough to go ice-skating.*

\* \* \*

*Knock knock.*
Who's there?
*Senior.*
Senior who?
*Senior uncle lately?*

\* \* \*

*Knock knock.*
Who's there?
*Senior.*
Senior who?
*Senior so nosey, I won't tell you.*

\* \* \*

*Knock knock.*
Who's there?
*Seymour.*

61

Seymour who?
*Seymour kittens out here.*

\* \* \*

*Knock knock.*
Who's there?
*Shad.*
Shad who?
*Shad up and open the door.*

\* \* \*

*Knock knock.*
Who's there?
*Sharon.*
Sharon who?
*Sharon share alike.*

\* \* \*

*Knock knock.*
Who's there?
*Sherwood.*
Sherwood who?
*Sherwood like for you to let me in.*

\* \* \*

*Knock knock.*
Who's there?
*Sherwood.*
Sherwood who?
*Sherwood like it if you'd let me kiss you.*

\* \* \*

*Knock knock.*
Who's there?
*Sherwood.*
Sherwood who?
*Sherwood like to hear another knock-knock joke.*

\* \* \*

*Knock knock.*
Who's there?
*Shirley.*
Shirley who?
*Shirley you must be joking.*

\* \* \*

*Knock knock.*
Who's there?
*Socket.*
Socket who?
*Socket to me!*

\* \* \*

*Knock knock.*
Who's there?
*Soda.*
Soda who?
*Soda you like me?*

\* \* \*

*Knock knock.*
Who's there?
*Sofa.*

Sofa who?
*Sofa, so good!*

\* \* \*

*Knock knock.*
Who's there?
*Sofa.*
Sofa who?
*Sofa you're doing fine.*

\* \* \*

*Knock knock.*
Who's there?
*Somber.*
Somber who?
*Somber over the rainbow.*

\* \* \*

*Knock knock.*
Who's there?
*Specter.*
Specter who?
*Specter Holmes of Scotland Yard.*

\* \* \*

*Knock knock.*
Who's there?
*Spinach.*
Spinach who?
*Spinaching me so long I had to scratch it.*

\* \* \*

*Knock knock.*
Who's there?
*Stan.*
Stan who?
*Stan aside — I'm coming through.*

\* \* \*

*Knock knock.*
Who's there?
*Stella.*
Stella who?
*Stella nother crazy knock-knock joke.*

\* \* \*

*Knock knock.*
Who's there?
*Sue.*
Sue who?
*Sue prize!*

\* \* \*

*Knock knock*
Who's there?
*Summertime.*
Summertime who?
*Summetime itsa hot, summertime itsa cold.*

\* \* \*

*Knock knock.*
Who's there?
*Summertime.*

Summertime who?
*Summertime I'm going to stop telling knock-knock jokes.*

* * *

*Knock knock.*
Who's there?
*Sum Toi.*
Sum Toi who?
*Sum Toi you've got there.*

* * *

*Would you know me if you didn't see me for a week?*
Sure!
*Would you know me if you didn't see me for a day?*
Sure!
*Knock knock.*
Who's there?
*See! You've forgotten me already.*

* * *

*Knock knock.*
Who's there?
*Swarm.*
Swarm who?
*Swarm enough to go swimming.*

* * *

*Knock knock.*
Who's there?
*Sweden.*
Sweden who?
*Sweden my tea with two lumps of sugar.*

\* \* \*

*Knock knock.*
Who's there?
*Taffilda.*
Taffilda who?
*Taffilda bucket you have to turn on the water.*

\* \* \*

*Knock knock.*
Who's there?
*Tamara.*
Tamara who?
*Tamara it's gonna rain.*

\* \* \*

*Knock knock.*
Who's there?
*Tara.*
Tara who?
*Tara-ra-boom-de-ay!*

\* \* \*

*Knock knock.*
Who's there?
*Tarzan.*
Tarzan who?
*Tarzan stripes forever.*

\* \* \*

*Knock knock.*

Who's there?
*Telly.*
Telly who?
*Telly Phone.*

\* \* \*

*Knock knock.*
Who's there?
*Thatcher.*
Thatcher who?
*Thatcher was a funny joke.*

\* \* \*

*Knock knock.*
Who's there?
*Thermos.*
Thermos who?
*Thermos be someone waiting who feels the way I do.*

\* \* \*

*Knock knock.*
Who's there?
*Thesis.*
Thesis who?
*Thesis a stickup!*

\* \* \*

*Knock knock.*
Who's there?
*Thistle.*
Thistle who?
*Thistle make you whistle.*

* * *

*Knock knock.*
Who's there?
*Thistle.*
Thistle who?
*Thistle be a lesson to me.*

* * *

*Knock knock.*
Who's there?
*Tom.*
Tom who?
*Tom-orrow is another day.*

* * *

*Knock knock.*
Who's there?
*Tomb.*
Tomb who?
*Tomb whom it may concern!*

* * *

*Knock knock.*
Who's there?
*Toucan.*
Toucan who?
*Toucan live as cheaply as one.*

* * *

*Knock knock.*

Who's there?
*Tuba.*
Tuba who?
*Tuba toothpaste.*

\* \* \*

*Knock knock.*
Who's there?
*Tulsa.*
Tulsa who?
*Tulsa story, please.*

\* \* \*

*Knock knock.*
Who's there?
*Turner.*
Turner who?
*Turner round. I can't stand your face.*

\* \* \*

*Knock knock.*
Who's there?
*Turnip.*
Turnip who?
*Turnip your pants at the bottom — they're too long.*

\* \* \*

*Knock knock.*
Who's there?
*Unawares.*
Unawares who?
*Unawares what you put on first every morning.*

*** 

*Knock knock.*
Who's there?
*Velvet.*
Velvet who?
*Velvet, how's my dog doing?*

* * *

*Knock knock.*
Who's there?
*Venice.*
Venice who?
*Venice your next birthday?*

* * *

*Knock knock.*
Who's there?
*Vera.*
Vera who?
*Vera interesting.*

* * *

*Knock knock.*
Who's there?
*Vicious.*
Vicious who?
*Vicious a Merry Christmas!*

* * *

*Knock knock.*

Who's there?
*Victor.*
Victor who?
*Victor his pants on the fence.*

* * *

*Knock knock.*
Who's there?
*Violet.*
Violet who?
*Violet you make these jokes I'll never understand.*

* * *

*Knock knock.*
Who's there?
*Wait a minute . . . you can't do a knock-knock joke!
those things went out of style years ago.*
Wait-a minute-you-can't-do a-knock-knock-joke-
those-things-went-out-of-style-years-ago WHO?

* * *

*Knock knock.*
Who's there?
*Warrant.*
Warrant who?
*Warrant you home before?*

* * *

*Knock knock.*
Who's there?
*Warren.*
Warren who?

*Warren Peace is a great Russian novel.*

* * *

*Knock knock.*
Who's there?
*Water.*
Water who?
*Water you doing?*

* * *

*Knock knock.*
Who's there?
*Weasel.*
Weasel who?
*Weasel while you work.*

* * *

*Knock knock.*
Who's there?
*Weed.*
Weed who?
*Weed better mow the lawn before it gets too long.*

* * *

*Knock knock.*
Who's there?
*Weevil.*
Weevil who?
*Weevil see you later.*

* * *

*Knock knock.*
Who's there?
*Wendy.*
Wendy who?
*Wendy joke is finished, you'd better laugh.*

* * *

*Knock knock.*
Who's there?
*Wilda.*
Wilda who?
*Wilda movie be on TV tonight?*

* * *

*Knock knock.*
Who's there?
*Wilfred.*
Wilfred who?
*Wilfred call me tonight?*

* * *

*Knock knock.*
Who's there?
*Winner.*
Winner who?
*Winner is when it snows.*

* * *

*Knock knock.*
Who's there?
*Wooden.*
Wooden who?

*Wooden nickel buy me that piece of candy?*

\* \* \*

*Knock knock.*
Who's there?
*Wooden.*
Wooden who?
*Wooden you like to go out with me?*

\* \* \*

*Knock knock.*
Who's there?
*Wren.*
Wren who?
*Wren are you coming out?*

\* \* \*

*Knock knock.*
Who's there?
*X.*
X who?
*X-tra, X-tra, read all about it!*

\* \* \*

*Knock knock.*
Who's there?
*You.*
You who?
*Yoo hoo, yourself.*

\* \* \*

*Knock knock.*
Who's there?
*You.*
You who?
*Are you calling me?*

\* \* \*

*Knock knock.*
Who's there?
*Yul.*
Yul who?
*Yul never know.*

\* \* \*

*Knock knock.*
Who's there?
*Zing.*
Zing who?
*Zing a song of sixpence . . . .*

\* \* \*

*Knock knock.*
Who's there?
*Zombies.*
Zombies who?
*Zombies make honey, and zombies just buzz around.*

\* \* \*

Some shun sunshine on Sundays.

* * *

What a shame such a shapely sash
should show shabby stitches.

* * *

Lean Linny Long loves Long Lenny Lean.

* * *

Luscious lemon liniment.

* * *

Strange strategic statistics.

* * *

Six shy soldiers sold seven salted salmons.

* * *

Sly Sam sips Sally's soup.

* * *

"Pucker, Pearl Potter, please," pleaded
Pete Perkins politely.

* * *

Two tree toads tied together tried to trot to town twice.

* * *

**The seething sea ceaseth seething.**

* * *

Sweet Suzie Skunk sells sugar shakers.

* * *

Geese cackle, cows moo, crows caw, cocks crow.

* * *

Beautiful babbling brooks bubble
between blossoming banks.

* * *

Of all the saws I ever saw saw,
I never saw a saw that saws as this saw saws.

* * *

"Hark, an aardvark!" Mark barked for a lark.

* * *

Rush the washing, Russell!

* * *

Four flat-backed fat blackbirds flew fitfully.

* * *

Toy boat.

\* \* \*

Pop dropped the slop mop when the cop stopped to hop.

\* \* \*

"Sleep, sleep, sleep," the slim shepherd
shouted sadly six times.

\* \* \*

Silver thimbles.

\* \* \*

Shipshape suit shops ship shapely suits.

\* \* \*

Round and round the rugged rock the ragged rascal ran.

\* \* \*

A shy little, she said "Shoo!" to a fly and a flea in a flue.

\* \* \*

Put pink paint in painted pots.

\* \* \*

Maybe baby bees bounce in baby buggy buggies.

\* \* \*

Soldiers' shoulders shudder when shrill shells shriek.

* * *

A critical cricket critic.

* * *

Who will wet the whetstone while Willie whistles wistfully?

* * *

Six shining soldiers.

* * *

Dick Hickey snickered niggardly, kicking sticky bricks.

* * *

Which wristwatches are Swiss wristwatches?

* * *

Sister Susie's sewing shirts for soldiers.

* * *

The girth of the earth giveth birth to mirth.

* * *

Seventy sailors sailed seven swift ships.

* * *

Sixty-six sickly chicks.

* * *

Goofy gophers gobble goodies gladly.

* * *

Silly Lily slithered slightly slyly, slowly slinging silver slivers.

* * *

Cows graze in groves on grass which grows
in grooves in groves.

* * *

Chilly Charlie Schilling surely chopped shallots and chives.

* * *

Six slippery, sliding snakes.

* * *

How many cans can a canner can if a canner can can cans?
A canner can can as many cans as a canner can if a canner
can can cans.

* * *

"Gee whiz, show biz," said Ms. Diz Fizz.

* * *

Eight angry alligators ate eight awful apricots.

* * *

Pete's pa, Pete, poked to the pea patch to pick a peck of peas for the poor pink pig in the pine hole pig pen.

* * *

Sally Wally dillydallies daily.

* * *

Good blood, bad blood.

* * *

This shop stocks short socks with stripes and spots.

* * *

Timmy Tomkins tripped Tommy Timkins.

* * *

Yellow yo-yos.

* * *

There is a pleasant peasant present.

* * *

Theda thought thick thickets thinned thoroughly.

* * *

The wild wolf roams the wintry wastes.

* * *

Busby Bee boldly buzzed by Benji Bear.

* * *

A real red rooster roosts in the rain.

* * *

Tuesday is stew day. Stew day is Tuesday.

* * *

"Jump, Judy, jump," Ginny Jenkins jabbered joyfully.

* * *

Let little Nellie run a little.

* * *

The sailor's tailor thoroughly failed furling.

* * *

Fat Mat Cat pats the rat in the hat.

* * *

If one doctor doctors another, does the doctor who doctors
the doctor doctor the doctor the way the doctor he is doc-

toring doctors? Or does he doctor the doctor the way the
doctor who doctors doctors?

\* \* \*

A bitter biting bittern bit a better brother bittern, and the
bitter better bittern bit the bitter biter back.
And the bitter bittern, bitten by the better bitten bittern,
said, "I'm a bitter biter bit, alack!"

\* \* \*

The big black-backed bumblebee.

\* \* \*

Double bubble gum bubbles double.

\* \* \*

Blue black bug's blood.

\* \* \*

A tall eastern girl named Short long loved a big Mr. Little.
But Little, thinking little of Short, loved a little lass
named Long.
To belittle Long, Short announced she would marry Little
before long.
This caused Little to shortly marry Long.
To make a long story short, did tall Short love big Little less
because Little loved little Long more?

\* \* \*

I never smelled a smelt that smelled as bad

as that smelt smelled.

* * *

Six selfish shellfish.

* * *

Plump Peter Panda picks pears, pecans, and pumpkins.

* * *

Georgia's gorge is gorgeous.

* * *

"Hi, Harry Healy," hollered Holly Heartley.

* * *

Fran fans Fred frantically.

* * *

Greek grapes are great.

* * *

Sure the ship's shipshape, sir.

* * *

Sheep shouldn't sleep in shaky shacks.
Sheep should sleep in sound sheds.

* * *

Fanny Finch fried five floundering fish for Francis's father.

\* \* \*

Six slick saplings.

\* \* \*

This is my sister's zither.

\* \* \*

Slim Sam shaved six slippery sideburns in six seconds.

\* \* \*

Nick nightly knocks knick-knacks.
No knick-knack knocker knocks knick-knacks like Nick.

\* \* \*

Beth believes thieves seize skis.

\* \* \*

Lotty licks lollies lolling in the lobby.

\* \* \*

Hairy Harry Hartley hurries home.

\* \* \*

While trying to whistle, Christopher Twistle

twisted his tongue.

* * *

Each Easter Eddie eats eighty Easter eggs.

* * *

Peter Porker picked pretty pink petunias.

* * *

Kiss her quickly! Kiss her quicker!

* * *

Sarah saw a shot-silk-sash shop full of snowy,
shiny shot-silk sashes.

* * *

Tie twine to three tree twigs.

* * *

Bisquick — Kiss quick!

* * *

She stood at the door of Mrs. Smith's fish-sauce shop.

* * *

Silly Sidney saves shoes, stools, and tools.

* * *

The sinking steamer.

* * *

She stood at the door of Burgess's fish-sauce
shop welcoming him in.

* * *

"Are you copper bottoming 'um, my man?"
"No, I'm aluminuming 'um, mum."

* * *

We shouted, "Swim, Swan, swim!"
The swan swam and swam back again.
"What a swim, Swan, you swam!"

* * *

Eleven enormous elephants elegantly eating Easter eggs.

* * *

Tho' a kiss be amiss,
She who misses the kisses,
As Miss without kiss,
May miss being Mrs.

* * *

Marsha rushed the crushed brush from the plush bush.

* * *

Wood said he would carry the wood through the wood.
And if Wood said he would, Wood would.

\* \* \*

Frivolous fat Fanny fried fresh fish furiously for four
famished Frenchmen.

\* \* \*

Mike borrows Ike's spikes to hike,
and Ike borrows Mike's bike.

\* \* \*

Sara saw a sash shop full of showy, shiny sashes.

\* \* \*

Seven silly skunks sighed sadly.

\* \* \*

As I went into the garden, I saw five brave maids sitting on
five broad beds braiding broad braids.
I said to these five brave maids sitting on five broad beds
braiding broad braids,
"Braid broad braids, brave maids."

\* \* \*

Glen's twin sisters sing tasteful tongue twisters.

\* \* \*

Every fall tall Paul Hall plays ball on the mall.

* * *

The sixth sheik's sixth sheep's sick.

* * *

Wheedling, weeping Winnie wails wildly.

* * *

The classy lass, aghast,
passed the last brass mast in the grass fast.

* * *

Shy Sheila shakes soft shimmering silks.

* * *

Thin tinsmith Tim thinks Tillie's thin twin thinks
Tim's twin thinner than Tillie's thin twin.

* * *

Little Glen Littler glibly glued limited
glittering glass globes.

* * *

His shirt soon shrank in the suds.

* * *

A cup of coffee in a copper coffeepot.

* * *

Charming, chic Charlotte chews choice,
cheap, chopped-cheese chips.

* * *

Does this shop stock short socks with spots?

* * *

Preshrunk shirts.

* * *

Cross crossings cautiously.

* * *

Unique New York.

* * *

Fat friars fanning flames.

* * *

Ten terrified tomcats tottering
in the tops of three tall trees.

* * *

She sewed shirts seriously.

* * *

Wiley Walter Rollins ran with Randy Watkins.

* * *

Tim, the thin twin tinsmith

* * *

Three tree twigs.

* * *

Six sick slick slim salmon swam swiftly south.

* * *

Shook's snapshot shop shall show
some sharp snapshots soon.

* * *

Six thick swamps.

* * *

When wicked witches whisk switches,
Which witch whisks switches swiftest?

* * *

Frank threw Fred three free throws.

* * *

Wise wives whistle while weaving worsted waistcoats.

\* \* \*

Ziggy Jazinski.

\* \* \*

Jack Jackson Zachary.

\* \* \*

Thrice times three, twice times two.

\* \* \*

Pokey Porky Porcupine pines for pretty Petunia Porker.

\* \* \*

Copper coffeepot.

\* \* \*

If Harry hurries, will hairy Henry hand him
a hundred hammers?

\* \* \*

A blue blank bankbook blew back of Blank's black bank.

\* \* \*

A big blue bucket of blue blueberries.

\* \* \*

Some think Tom Thumb's plumb dumb.

* * *

Pink peas please plump porkers.

* * *

I said, "a knapsack strap," not "a knapsack's strap."

* * *

Rapidly Red read what Net wrote in red watercolor.

* * *

Six silly sisters sell silk to six sickly seniors.

* * *

Swift Sam Smith said Shifty Sidney Smithers
shouldn't send silly signals.

* * *

Six gray geese on green grass grazing.

* * *

Six silent snakes slithering slowly southward.

* * *

Both boats brought broad boards. Ross boarded both boats,
bought broad boards both boasts brought.

* * *

An antiquated ape ate eighty-eight apples
and ate eight assassinated ants also.

\* \* \*

Five French friars fanning a fainted flea.

\* \* \*

Shell-shocked soldiers shiveringly shrug shoulders
selling shrapnel souvenirs to sailors.

\* \* \*

Wiley Rocky really wrote "Rocket" rottenly.

\* \* \*

A skunk jumped over a stump in a skunk hole.

\* \* \*

A lively young fisher named Fischer
Fished for fish from the edge of a fissure.
A fish with a grin pulled the fisherman in!
Now they are hunting the fissure for Fischer.

\* \* \*

Ten tiny turtles talk to twenty timid toads.

\* \* \*

Sly Sheila Slem said she saw sixty-six slick
shoeshine shops' signs shine.

\* \* \*

Lightning bugs blaze bright at night, right?

\* \* \*

Sixteen sad sacks sitting side by side.

\* \* \*

Ned Nott was shot and Sam Shott was not.
So it is better to be Shott than Nott.
Some say Nott was not shot.
But Shott says he shot Nott.
Either the shot Shott shot at Nott was not shot,
Or Nott was shot.
If the shot Shott shot shot Nott, Nott was shot.
But if the shot Shott shot shot Shott,
Then Shott was shot, not Nott.
However, the shot Shott shot shot not Shott — but Nott.

\* \* \*

A noisy noise annoys an oyster.

\* \* \*

What a pity poor Peter pecked pretty Polly's pigs.

\* \* \*

Ready Freddy Fox flicks fleas furiously.

\* \* \*

The skunk sat on a stump and thunk the stump stunk.
But the stump thunk the skunk stunk.

* * *

Lazy Larry Llama loves lovely Lucy Lion.

* * *

Naughty Nettie's knitting knotted nighties for the navy.

* * *

Dauntless Dan Dudley does daring dives daily.

* * *

Benny Butler bought bitter butter in a brass bell
but broke it.

* * *

The bootblack brought the book back.

* * *

She says she sews silk shoe soles,
So she surely shall save shoes.

* * *

Shave a thin cedar shingle.

* * *

Six slippery seals slipping silently ashore.

* * *

A cup of proper coffee in a copper coffee cup.

* * *

Davy Dear ducks Dinah Dear daily.

* * *

Frances Fowler's father fried five floundering flounder for
Frances Fowler's father's father.

* * *

Bold Bingo Bunny bounced badly.

* * *

Dirty Danny Dog didn't dig dirt, did he?

* * *

Bonnie Bliss blows big beautiful blue bubbles.

* * *

Fast Freddie Frog fries fat flying fish.

* * *

Lucky Louie Lion likes licking lemon lollipops.

* * *

Literally literary literature.

* * *

Sister Sue's silly song is softly sweet.

* * *

Nine nimble noblemen nibble nuts.

* * *

How many bagels could a beagle bake
If a beagle could bake bagels?

* * *

Windy weather makes Wendy Worm wiggle wildly.

* * *

Blame the big bleak black book!

* * *

Tuesday Timmy told two tall tales to Tommy Tucker.

* * *

"Hark! An ark lark!" barked Bart.

* * *

She says she shall sew a sheet.

* * *

If you stick a stick across a stick,
Or stick a cross across a stick,
Or cross a stick across a stick,
Or stick a cross across a cross,
Or cross a cross across a stick,
Or cross a cross across a cross,
Or stick a crossed stick across a stick,
Or stick a crossed stick across a crossed stick,
Or cross a crossed stick across a cross,
Or cross a crossed stick across a crossed stick,
Would that be an acrostic?

\* \* \*

A queer quick questioning quiz.

\* \* \*

A big black bug bit a big black bear.
Where is the big black bear the big black bug bit?

\* \* \*

Seth hoes Beth's rows.

\* \* \*

Miss Smith dismisseth us.

\* \* \*

Ron Watts runs rat races.

\* \* \*

Wee Willy whistles to wise Wilber Whale.

* * *

Thin sticks, thick bricks.

* * *

Shrewd Si sold soled shoes Simple Simon sewed.
Simple Simon sewed soled shoes Shrewd Si sold.
If Shrewd Si sold soled shoes Simple Simon sewed,
Where are the sewed soled shoes Shrewd Si sold?

* * *

Monday morning mother made mincemeat pies.

* * *

A bootblack blacks boots with a black blacking brush.

* * *

Bob's job's to rob gobs of fobs.

* * *

Pure food for four pure mules.

* * *

Pretty pink pigs pile pea pods on paper plates.

* * *

Flesh of fresh flying fish.

\* \* \*

Six twin-screw cruisers.

\* \* \*

Slippery southern snakes slide swiftly down ski slopes.

\* \* \*

Old, oily Ollie oils oily autos.

\* \* \*

Penny Park passes peas to Patty Perkins.

\* \* \*

Slim Sam slid sideways.

\* \* \*

Sad Sam Smither's in a dither about Sid Withers.

\* \* \*

The mixer fixer nixed her elixir.

\* \* \*

"Bye, bye, bluebird," Billy Beaver bellowed.

\* \* \*

Don't run along the wrong lane!

* * *

Why whine when wine whets a withered vine?

* * *

I saw Esau kissing Kate.
I saw Esau, he saw me.
And she saw I saw Esau.

* * *

"Shoot, Sally," Slim Sam shouted shyly.

* * *

Surely the sun shall shine soon.

* * *

Cheap ship trips.

* * *

Silly Suzy Simpkins sees shapely Cindy Shore.

* * *

This is a zither.

* * *

Happy Henry Hippo hops over a high hill humming.

* * *

Fast Frank fires frankfurters and French fries.

* * *

Peggy Babcock.

* * *

Meek Morgan Matthews made weak Matty Morgan
many milkshakes.

* * *

A ship saileth south soon.

* * *

"Whose shoe?" sighed Sue.
"My shoe," lied Lou.
"Here's your shoe, Lou," cried Sue.
"Shucks, Sue, thank you," Lou sighed.
"My shoe!" cried Blue. "I'll sue Lou and Sue!"

* * *

Bill had a billboard. Bill also had a board bill.
The board bill bored Bill, so that Bill sold the billboard to
pay his board bill.
So after Bill sold his billboard to pay his board bill, the
board bill no longer bored Bill.

* * *

Lisbeth lisps lengthy lessons.

* * *

Saving Susie Shaw saws shingles and saves shavings.
Shy sister Sadie Shaw sells sawed shingles and saved shavings saving Susie Shaw saves.

\* \* \*

Peter Prangle, the prickly pear pickler, picked three pecks
of prickly Prangle pears from the Prangle pear trees of the
pleasant prairies.

\* \* \*

If a Hottentot taught a Hottentot tot to talk e'er the tot
could totter,
Ought the Hottentot tot be taught to say aught, or naught,
Or what ought to be taught her?

\* \* \*

If to hoot and to toot a Hottentot tot be taught by a
Hottentot tutor,
Should the tutor get hot if the Hottentot tot hoot and toot
at the Hottentot tutor?

\* \* \*

If a woodchuck could chuck wood, how much wood could a
woodchuck chuck if a woodchuck could chuck wood? He
would chuck, he would, as much as he could, if a woodchuck could chuck wood.

\* \* \*

A tooter who tooted a flute tried to tutor two tutors to toot.
Said the two to the tutor, "Is it harder to toot or to tutor
two tutors to toot?"

* * *

"A pox on your flocks," said the fox on the rocks.

* * *

I need not your needles, they're needless to me,
For needing needles is needless, you see.
But did my neat trousers but need to be kneed,
I then should have need of your needles indeed.

* * *

A maid with a duster made a furious bluster,
Dusting a bust in the hall.
When the bust it was dusted,
The bust it was busted,
The bust it was dust, that's all.

* * *

Who washed Washington's woolen winter underwear when
Washington's wonderful washerwoman went west?

* * *

The crow flew over the river with a lump
of raw liver in his mouth.

* * *

Seventy shuddering sailors standing silent as short, sharp,
shattering shocks shake their splendid ship.

* * *

Betty Botter bought some butter.
But she said, "The butter's bitter.
If I put it in my batter,
It will make my batter bitter.
But a bit of better butter —
That would make my batter better."
So she bought a bit of butter
Better than her bitter butter.
And she put it in her batter,
And the batter was not bitter.
So 'twas better Betty Botter
Bought a bit of better butter.

* * *

Terrance Thyllis tallied Tillie's tennis team's tally.

* * *

Tall Tommy Tortoise talked to Tillie Turtle
on the telephone ten times today.

* * *

Joe jumps joyfully in June and July.

* * *

Rubber baby buggy bumpers.

* * *

Industrious Dessie dexterously dusts dusty desks daily.

* * *

A tree toad loved a she-toad that lived up in a tree.
She was a three-toed tree toad, but a two-toed toad was he.
The two-toed toad tried to win the she-toad's friendly nod,
For the two-toed toad loved the ground
on which the three-toad toad trod.
But no matter how the two-toed tree toad tried,
he could not please her whim.
In her tree-toad bower, with her three-toed power,
the she-toad vetoed him.

* * *

Sensible, sensitive Selma Sell seldom sells shellfish.

* * *

Lanny, lately addled, ladled only lowly lentils.

* * *

Mr. See owned a saw and Mr. Soar owned a seesaw.
Now See's saw sawed Soar's seesaw before Soar saw See,
Which made Soar sore.
Had Soar seen See's saw before See sawed Soar's seesaw,
See's saw would not have sawed Soar's seesaw.
So See's saw sawed Soar's seesaw.
But it was a shame to see Soar so sore just because
See's saw sawed Soar's seesaw.

* * *

Herr Hurd hurt his head as he herded his herd.
Herr Hurd's heir, airing her hair,
Heard Herr Hurd err ere Herr Hurd heard her.

\* \* \*

Hairy Harry Hound hurries home.

\* \* \*

Mack Yak packs sacks.

\* \* \*

Barbara burned the brown bread badly.

\* \* \*

Two timid toads trying to tickle ten trout.

\* \* \*

Pitter-patter, pitter-patter,
rather than patter-pitter, patter-pitter.

\* \* \*

Pass Polly pizza, please.

\* \* \*

Pete piles pink pails on pewter pots.

\* \* \*

Hairy Henry Hippo hopped happily.

\* \* \*

The chump jumped a stump, went bump, and got a lump.

\* \* \*

Blue Billy Bradley butters bread badly.

\* \* \*

If a weary witch wished a weird wish
with a withered wizard's whip,
Where is the withered wizard's whip
with which the weary witch wished?

\* \* \*

She sawed six slick sleek slim slender saplings.

\* \* \*

Sad Sam Smith smuggles saltwater seashells.

\* \* \*

Six thick thistle sticks.

\* \* \*

Three terrible thieves.

\* \* \*

Little Linda Lamb licks her lovely lips.

* * *

Friendly Freda Fly flips flapjacks.

* * *

Billy Bunny burst his big, beautiful, blue balloon.

* * *

Silly Suzy Sharp saved sharp Sidney Smith.

* * *

"Ginny Jenkins jumped joyfully," Jenny Johnson jeered.

* * *

Esther Elephant eats eighty-eight Easter eggs eagerly.

* * *